THE LEADER'S
BLUEPRINT

HOW AVERAGE LEADERS BECOME ALPHAS
...AND WHY *YOU* SHOULD TOO

TERRY T. BUDGET
FOREWORD BY RADM. REUBIN BOOKERT
United States Navy (Retired)

i

Published by Lee's Press and Publishing Company
www.LeesPress.net

All rights reserved, Except for brief excerpts for review purposes, no part of this book may be reproduced or used in any form without written permission from Terry T. Budget and/or the publisher.

This document is published by Lee's Press and Publishing Company located in the United States of America. It is protected by the United States Copyright Act, all applicable state laws and international copyright laws. The information in this document is accurate to the best of the ability of Terry T. Budget at the time of writing. The content of this document is subject to change without notice.

To book Terry for speaking engagements, coaching or consulting please go to:

www.TerryBudget.com

ISBN-13: 978-0999310380 *Paperback*
ISBN-10: 0999310380

ACKNOWLEDGEMENTS

SFC Alphonso B. Dawson (deceased) - My first military supervisor who gave me the visual concept of what a leader should be and how to make others laugh with me.

SGM Ricky L. Douglas - My old junior Non-Commissioned Officer and right hand who let me know when I was failing as a leader. Thanks for all the instructions and sideline talks.

CSM (retired) Neil Ciotola – The epitome of a military leader. Our talks became a great inspiration to me. Thanks for the motivation!

SGM Levi Bennett - Thanks for teaching me the leadership concept that you don't have to raise your voice to get things done. You are a great role model.

Dawn Nicole – An incredible business strategist. Your ideas and practices took me in directions I never thought possible. I love your mind. Change the world one company at a time!

Dr. Myles Munroe (deceased) - Although we've never met, your teachings were the cornerstone of my understanding of what leadership truly means. Rest in

Peace!

Terry C. McFadden – Thank you for all your support in writing this book and standing by me while I chased my dreams.

DEDICATION

To my **Creator** and **King** – There is no me without You. Thank You for your blessings and empowering me to write this book. I know that because Your fingerprint is on it, it will change leaders for the better.

To **Jennie B. Garcia** – My mother, advisor, teacher, and confidant. Thank you for believing in me and supporting my goals. You are truly my best friend. I love you!

To **Eva L. Budget** - The best grandmother a young man could ever have. You are the cornerstone and backbone of the family. Because of your love and prayers, this book became a reality. You are my heart!

FOREWORD

It is important to understand that leadership has been described and perceived by various experts in the field of business, philosophy, and in life as an ability that is demonstrated through action. As a United States Navy Admiral, I have had the privilege to serve my country and be a leader over many individuals, but after reading this book, I discovered a new level of understanding and respect for the word "leadership" and its application. Its application of the mind.

As you look within yourself and ponder who you really are at the core, you alone must ask yourself if you know what it means to be a leader. I don't mean just an average leader because the world has plenty of those. I'm talking about the exceptional leader...the Alpha! How well are you performing as a leader in your organization? Are you empowering other people to become better than they believe they can be?

Regardless of how you have answered these questions, you're going to want to read this book for even greater clarity. Why? You already know that leadership is about influence and making things happen, but what you don't know is to what depth this concept is really immersed. I'm referring to the level of thinking. This idea includes the attributes which are needed to be successful in making a difference in the world through leadership...*Your Leadership!*

The Leader's Blueprint creates a structure that doesn't just explain what the Alpha is, but also how to become it. We are the directors of our destiny and the master of our minds. We are the ones who must decide what kind of leader we want to be and how we will guide others into becoming exceptional leaders. This book sets the stage for your mind and outlines the design to achieve that goal.

Terry has poured his heart and soul into this writing and I'm certain that those who incorporate its content will discover their hidden leadership potential and affect change on a massive scale. His years in military service, especially in combat environments, along with his academic studies from multiple institutions of higher learning allowed him to experience leadership perspectives through personal action and close observation of other leaders... making him an authority on this topic.

As an eloquent keynote speaker and author, Terry has combined the pillars that compose the philosophy of true leadership and expresses it in a comprehensive work that is easy to read and ready to put into immediate action by transforming the mind through implementing its leadership principles.

Start today by reading, learning, understanding, and applying the information he has provided with this accumulation of leadership knowledge. There is an Alpha inside of you waiting to be discovered and Terry has given you the blueprint...The Leader's Blueprint.

Reubin Bookert
Rear Admiral
United States Navy
(Retired)

PREFACE

When I started to implement the ideas in this book, my whole life changed. I was unaware that I had attained so much information about a specific area of knowledge. I never imagined in a million years that I would actually be writing a book about it. However, I do believe that my thoughts, ideas, and perspectives can be best illustrated in words. For this reason, I wanted to ensure that a pathway can be created for new and emerging leaders in today's era.

I believe that the philosophy that is presented in this book can be enacted immediately. Some perspectives will be familiar, and some new. All of them have the power to catapult your mind and actions into results, no matter how high you're trying to aim. I've held nothing back which means that at times you may find yourself slightly looking at your own points of view in a way that may be in contrast with mine. It would be difficult for me to just tell you what I think or what I believe. I can only tell you what I've lived.

Transforming from a follower to a leader was not an easy course. Living as a timid child, I had to learn the hard way. Thanks to service in the military, I learned what aspects of being a leader was all about.

The interesting thing about leadership in the military is that it was multi-dimensional, but with a singular path. In comparison to my life back home, experiences during my school years and my environment, I never thought I would be where I am today as a keynote speaker on leadership and now an author.

I know that the Creator has placed in me the wisdom, knowledge, and understanding needed to express the principles and applications I have learned through many years of both studies, successes, and failures into a comprehensive, yet digestible work to guide new and emerging leaders towards becoming better and more effective industry influencers. I want you, the reader, to become….the ALPHA!

To those entering leadership, I hope this book helps you make a difference in your people, your organization, and the world. More importantly, I hope it helps to change "YOU" for the better. If you want to transform the world, you must first, transform your mind!

God Bless,

Terry

Who This Book Is For

The focus of this book is on new and emerging leaders of organizations; those who aspire to become industry influencers, those who aspire to attain leadership roles, and those who are now assuming the supervisory role of others. Its core is to create a mindset for these leaders and is intended to provide a foundational design for them to become an ALPHA... *The Exceptional Leader*!

Although many books have been written to express the style and actions of an Alpha, this writing is meant to capture the essence of the Alpha spirit and philosophy. Additionally, this book will be of great value to leadership developers, trainers, and coaches whose focus is on building the 21st century generation of leaders within their current organizations.

We are facing a new generation filled with millennial's and this generation must be guided and empowered to conceive innovative ideas directed by a leadership blueprint. The next generation of leaders will need wisdom and experience if they are going to excel and take organizations to the next level. The information contained herein is also a positive reinforcement tool for managers and supervisors at all levels. Not limited to corporations, it provides independent and collaborative thinking for leaders of churches, non-profits, educational institutions, foundations, and associations. Unlike many other leadership books, this content primarily focuses on the mindset, and not just the processes.

How to Use This Book

The content of this book is meant to be used not just as reading material, but also as a mental leadership outline. It has been divided into multiple chapters to express and expand the A.L.P.H.A. philosophy- **A**ttitude, **L**eadership, **P**urpose, **H**onor, and **A**cumen. If you are serious about transforming yourself from an average leader to an exceptional leader and willing to put in the time and effort to do so, then you must understand the pillars of this philosophy and apply them daily. This learning pathway is a continuous journey to be traveled, not a destination.

Nothing is initiated, processed, resolved, or completed without effective leadership. Leadership is a team sport, not a solo act. The world needs exceptional leaders, but so few are willing to walk the path. They are needed at all levels and in all functions of an organization. You and your colleagues must become the best leaders possible and lead with brilliance, with rigor, and with tenacity. They need you to become... the *ALPHA*! Your exceptional leadership is required not only for today; but for tomorrow and in the future. Leadership is not about doing, but more so about becoming. When you transform your mind, you transform your actions. Others are inspired by leaders who know their purpose and are motivated by their passions, but more so because they know who they are and where they are going.

Keep this book readily accessible to you and refer to it when you have questions about your own level of leadership thinking, competency, and actions. All people, regardless of their leadership position, supervisory capacity, or management level who are seeking to become new leaders, can use this as a foundational design to spearhead awareness for themselves and their teams. Just as Luke Skywalker learned the ways of the force in Star Wars, so you, as a new or emerging leader, must learn the ways of the ALPHA!

TABLE OF CONTENTS

CHAPTER #1

ATTITUDE 2
    You Are What You Eat 6
    Focus or Flatline.. 13
    Pyramid of Character................................. 17
    Clear Your Mind of "Can't" 22
    Feel the Heat 24

CHAPTER #2

LEADERSHIP 28
    The Lynch Pin.. 32
    The "Connection" Infection 35
    Power through Empowering 43
    You are ALWAYS on Stage 48
    ....
    The Diversity Effect.................................... 52
    You Can't Dunk on Me 57

CHAPTER #3

PURPOSE 63
    Why Me? 65
    Create Your Value....................................... 68
    Problems, Problems, Problems 72
    Close Your Eyes...Open Your Mind 76

CHAPTER #4

HONOR 82
    Way of the Warrior 84
    Your Name Will Go Further Than You 88
    The Fish Rots from the Head 90
    Walk Hard or Go Home 94

CHAPTER #5

ACUMEN 99
    Arm Yourself for Battle............................ 102
    Don't You Trust Me? 106
    Hold 'em or Fold 'em 112
    Decisions for Decades 115

CHAPTER #6

Calling All ALPHAs! 120

INTRODUCTION

What is the ALPHA?

The ALPHA is the exceptional leader who exemplifies the idea of how a person expresses themselves in thought and action. Throughout this writing, you will learn and understand why the Alpha is the epitome of all leaders. Everyone was born to lead, but we must become the leader that we were born to be through a process. To become the exceptional leader, the *ALPHA*, we must embody what it actually takes to become it. This is not just an action plan or technique, but a mindset. Don't be misled into believing that the Alpha is just for the male. In truth, the Alpha is both genders. You are the orchestrator of your own destiny and your own way of thinking. Regardless of previous experiences or beliefs, you too can become exceptional.

The strength of the Alpha mentality hinges on five principle pillars: Attitude, Leadership, Purpose, Honor, and Acumen. The pillars of this mindset denote the Alpha belief system. Although anyone can and should become an Alpha, most will not. Only you know if you are capable of it, so don't let anyone define who you are or who you can be. This book will explain in detail a developmental process of thinking, acting, and communicating that advances leader's self-awareness and their ability to inspire those around them to become exceptional. The goal is not simply to fix things you do, but to transform the way you think. Your change in thinking will change your habits. Leadership is not what you do, but rather who you are. It is a journey of self-discovery. Don't look for your leadership in external places around you. It is in a place where you can't miss it...*within you!*

CHAPTER 1

ATTITUDE

"Attitude is a little thing that makes a big difference"

- Winston Churchill

ATTITUDE

Alpha's are very unique people. They have a very unique distinction, that is, that their thinking is different. Alphas do not think like average leaders. In fact, they use to be average. There was a certain transformation that took place in their mind and this transformation caused them to think differently. In most cases, it was an experience or event that took place that caused this change. However; whatever it was, it caused a significant change in the perception of how they see themselves and the world. This change embodied a new belief system. I call it, *the Alpha attitude*.

The Alpha has a belief system that places him or her above the average leader. Excellence is no longer the goal. The goal is to be EXCEPTIONAL. The Alpha understands that leadership is not based on fear, but on a high degree of respect and integrity. This belief system is called attitude and it causes the Alpha to act based on what they think. When developing the Alpha attitude, the leader understands that it is the mind that determines whether they are excellent or exceptional. It is their unique attitude that distinguishes the Alpha from average leaders. This attitude produces certain behaviors that stretches the Alpha beyond the norm. It is the discernment of the Alpha that makes them see circumstances differently than the average leader. The Alpha interprets problems and solutions differently from all others. They also see problems as opportunities to excel and grow. In other words, they teach others to become Alphas.

Attitude is a product of belief. The Alpha is an extraordinary leader simply because of what he or she believes about him or herself. The world for each of us is what we think it is. There is a correspondence between the things we see, hear, touch, taste, and smell, but we look at them from different standpoints... *our* standpoint. Each day millions of men and women enter the workforce with a certain attitude usually determined by a recent event or something that stroked a particular chord. To some, the workforce is a great place to be while others view it as a place of bondage. Their mundane existence in the workplace is simply that way because they believe it is so. With this attitude, can you alter the circumstances of your world or do you accept and interpret it purely on the current situation? The Alpha does not concern himself with such thinking.

How does the Alpha change their attitude? The simple answer is this; by learning to control their thoughts. The fear-thought doesn't have to make you afraid; the anger-thought doesn't have to make you angry. Control your attitude and in turn, you can control your world. Attitude can fill you with hope, or plunge you into despair; can fill you with inspiration or crush all initiative; can make you persevere against any obstacles, or create challenges to impede your every step. Your thoughts can make you or unmake you. By changing your attitude, you make the life you seek in business or in life possible.

New leaders who desire to become Alphas understand that raising awareness of self is only a singular aspect of becoming an exceptional leader. They must also improve the condition of others and their attitude. You must cultivate the mental attitude, *"I'm here to make a difference and I want to always improve myself and others. I want to know the keys to a positive attitude and I'm going to master its secrets."* The question is, "What are the secrets?

THE SECRETS

You Are What You Eat

"We become what we think about" - **Earl Nightingale**

Organizations spend billions of dollars annually to send their managers and executives to leadership development courses. Yes, that's billions with a "B". They return to the organization with new and interesting skills, tools, processes, and systems to use that they believe is either the current trend or the hottest program. The problem is, it's all the manager and leader receives. Nothing really changes mentally about *"them"*. Leadership development has been understood to reflect new actions, new processes and new systems, but seldom does it ever promote new thinking. If you want to change the world, you must change what you think about it and how you see it. In short, focus less on technique and more on thinking. This is true leadership development.

Earl Nightingale did an audio recording called, *The Strangest Secret*. In it he stated, "We become what we think about." In essence, what we believe in our subconscious mind is what we become. Although this may seem like a simple action, it can become complex. The mind is filled with many ideas and we feed it what we want to. We are what we eat. The problem lies in what we feed it. Often, we engorge our minds with positive and negative things without distinguishing between the two. The challenge, however; is to determine what needs to stay and what needs to go.

As new leaders, it is necessary to learn what needs to be digested in the mind. Your subconscious mind is wise and retains all data, but it will not argue with what you feed it nor will it challenge what you believe. As a leader in an organization, you must determine what information you deposit and how you will use it based on what you have been fed. When you're seeking an answer to a problem, your subconscious will respond, but it expects you to come to a decision and to take action in your conscious mind. If you want your subconscious mind to work for you, feed it properly.

New leaders have the power to choose what they feed their mind, but what happens all too often is they are interrupted by external forces like older leaders with systematic thinking, past processes, resistance to change from co-workers, etc. This interference results in the new leader not accepting positive information into the subconscious mind because it conflicts with the organizational norm or what they have been taught to believe. Although feeding the mind the positive information it needs to be innovative, finding it isn't always easy. Furthermore, retraining the current thinking of a new leader can become a monumental task. Procuring information from multiple sources is a good thing, but what is a *good* thing isn't always the *right* thing. To change a new leader's reality, they must change their mentality.

The secret is to understand the culture of the organization and its industry, what its vision is for the future, and what its values are in relation to that of the new leader and finally to be a student of leadership itself. Creativity, innovation, and competency are critical to assuming a new position, but it can only flourish when the leader enters it with an open mind, knowledge of the organization practices, a clearly defined vision, and a positive attitude. To possess a positive attitude, the mind must be fed the right information to transform thinking. Ideas are everywhere. Information is everywhere. New leaders must go in search of new ideas that challenge the normal way of doing things. They must become thought leaders.

Thought leadership is the epic trend of today's society and the focus of the Alpha mind. Having the right attitude propels one's ability to think and generate positive results. To generate and expand thoughts, new leaders must surround themselves with those who are focused and embrace what I call "stratospheric thinking". Stratospheric thinking is the conceptual idea that elevates a leader's consciousness to expand past what is practical or common and touch the outer reaches of what appears to be impossible. These thought leaders think not in terms of, "Is this even possible?", but instead, "Even this is possible".

In his book, *177 Mental Toughness Secrets of the World Class,* Steve Siebold wrote, "Middle Class performers are stuck in a mindset that knowledge is power, when the truth is that intelligent use of knowledge is and always has been the true power." What the mind is fed will determine what is possible for the leader. This is not new information for an Alpha. Those thoughts are projected to the organization and can affect outcomes of corporate goals. New leaders develop new attitudes when they encounter new information, in addition to, higher awareness of themselves and those around them. They continue to feed themselves information that elevates their consciousness and permits them to be innovative. Exceptional leaders truly are what they eat and new leaders know they must either focus on innovation or flatline in stagnation.

So how do you eat the right thing and feed your mind? First, be aware of who you are letting into your head. Too often leaders listen to others who express their opinion about a situation, but clearly have never been faced with that situation or similar situations. Therefore, all they have is a thought with no solid experience. New leaders must surround themselves with others who are experienced and can challenge their thinking. That person will not tell you what to do, but help you find alternatives to solve the problem. They will help you to think because your association will determine your destination.

Next, be selective in what you read. Learning material comes in all forms and is great to keep the mind occupied off of daily distracting activities. However, what you read should be in line with your goals and vision. As a new leader, what you think is expressed by what you say and how you act. Books have as much influence as people. The more you read information that is in line with what you believe, the more what you believe will be openly revealed to others. What you choose to read should advance your intellect and empower others. In *The Power of the Subconscious Mind,* Dr. Joseph Murphy wrote, "...it is not the thing that is believed in that hurts or harms you, but the believe or thought of the mind which create the result."

Speak positive words to yourself and to the team regularly. What enters the conscious mind repetitively will be digested into the subconscious. What you speak and hear regularly will trigger what the mind believes. Encourage others around you to seek higher levels of awareness or education to evolve their level of understanding. Speak up for what is ethical and represents you and the organization positively in the public eye.

Finally, remain up to date on the events that are happening around you. As a new leader, you not only want to know what is happening in your organization and your team, but also the events of the world that could affect the direction or interests of the organization. The more informed you are, the more valuable you become. Keep others informed as well because what you feed your mind can also feed theirs. Leaders, especially Alphas, are always learning. Ken Blanchard and Mark Miller, authors of *Great Leaders Grow* wrote, "The capacity to learn determines the capacity to lead. If you stop learning, you stop leading." Continue to feed your mind with as much positive information as you can because you truly are what you eat.

Provoking Question:

What are your feeding your mind?

Focus or Flatline

"The mind's direction is more important that its progress" – **Joseph Joubert**

French poet, Victor Hugo said, "No army can withstand the strength of an idea whose time has come". Ideas come and go, but as a leader, it is necessary to consider multiple ideas and make determinations on its validity relative to the organization's goals. No matter how bizarre an idea may seem, it is often the out-of-the-box thinking that generates a larger return. Why? Usually because it is something that the average leader would not consider viable relative to the current goals. Leaders, especially Alphas consider nothing to far-fetched.

Alpha's focus on the big picture without dismissing the details. As a new leader emerges, logical thought must give way to new possibilities. The mind of a leader must have laser-like focus without ignoring the bigger picture. Consider a machine gunner who fires sporadically at a target. The objective is to kill everything within a given area with the assumption that anything at all will be hit with the rounds. Now consider a sniper who has a specialized rifle with a scope. The target is specific and the strike point is very precise. The details of the shot are calculated and meticulous and nothing is left to chance. The sniper motto is, "One Shot, One Kill".

Focus is the steering wheel of an exceptional leader. The leader knows that if there is no focus in a specific direction to achieve a goal, then all roads lead to nowhere. Let's take it to an even deeper level. The new leader who wishes to become exceptional doesn't devote all their energy on *doing*, but more so on *becoming*. Only a foolish leader tries to be perfect. They know they can only strive to become better each day and there is always something new to learn. Further, the concept is what got them here today will not keep them here. So, they must always focus on becoming better and empowering others to become better because every action must be intentional and deliberate to achieve a goal.

The heartbeat of any organization is its people. If the heart doesn't beat, you get a flatline. Flatlining is not an option for a leader, or at least, it shouldn't be. Recognizing that individual focus apart from the team effort will only lead to confusion, misunderstanding, resistance and ultimately flatlining. Supervisors and managers focus on the systems and circumstances while Alphas focus on the people. So, you ask, "Why focus on the people and not the end-result?" Teams understand that the objective of the company is important and they know they play a role in that accomplishment. As a new leader, it is imperative that you identify and understand people's behaviors, motivations, skill sets, and mindsets because they are the ones who will cause the success or failure of a goal. Guess what...you, as the new leader, accepts the responsibility of what happens or fails to happen in that endeavor. Listen and focus on what your team is telling you. As a new leader, if you fail to focus, you could be a heartbeat away from flatlining.

Alphas are focused listeners and seek to understand the thoughts, ideas, opinions and feelings of others. With this in mind, an exceptional leader can determine where the focus of their people is and what they need to do to make adjustments for their own betterment, as well as, that of their colleagues. People are walking encyclopedias and they hold a wealth of information that is available within the space of a single heartbeat.

Exceptional leaders focus on the heartbeat of the people and the organization's direction. They refuse to allow themselves or anyone else to flatline as long as they can do something to prevent it. Sometimes leaders must step back and take advantage of assuming a neutral position between executives, senior leaders, colleagues, and subordinates in efforts to obtain a clear perspective of information.

Steve Chandler, author of *The Hands-off Manager* wrote, "Many people think that being focused in this neutral, accepting way makes them passionless and directionless managers. Quite the opposite! Pure action emerges from an undistracted mind." Clear thoughts allow the creation of solid plans and prevent tainted actions.

Provoking Question:

Are you focused on the people or the processes?

Pyramid of Character

"Knowledge will give you power, but character...respect!"
- Bruce Lee

How often do you change? Are your consistent? Are you predictable? Are you the same person all the time? One of the most important aspects about leadership is ones' character. A person with character does not act on what is popular, but what is principled. This is one of the reasons why many politicians today lack a degree of character. Politics is based on popularity and this can interfere with the quality of their character. This does not imply that politicians are without character, but it does provide validity to the point that some will sacrifice character for that popularity.

New and emerging leaders must have unwavering character because people will not follow who they do not trust. Character attracts loyalty. International speaker, seminar leader and author, Francis Hesselbein wrote in her book, *Hesselbein on Leadership*, *"Young people are looking for evidence of values-driven leadership because they see to many examples of people in positions of authority who are self-serving, focused only on financial lines, or simply indifferent to others."* Chances are that even in today's corporate society, we seldom find leaders who embody the principles that create a solid model of character. This is due in part because there may not exist a blueprint in the organization's hierarchy to illustrate how it should be. What is written in an organization's mission or vision statement may be contrary to what is demonstrated in their daily culture.

Character is a commitment to a set of values without compromise. It is a dedication to a set of moral standards that promote a leaders' actions. Character in a truly exceptional leader is very subtle, but makes a profound impact. They have self-imposed discipline that distinguishes them from the average leader. The late Dr. Miles Munroe, pastor of Bahamas Faith Ministry and renowned leadership speaker said, *"A person of character locks themselves up in the prison of their own convictions."* This refers to the premise that a leader's moral value restricts them to acting accordingly to what they believe is right. These moral values and belief system are always consistent and defines an individual's character. This character is projected through a leader's attitude. The Alpha prides themselves on their character because they understand that character is their pyramid. If you ever study the ancient pyramids of Egypt, you will notice that through thousands of years since their construction, they have not changed. Even through violent environmental conditions or human excavation, they have withstood the test of time. They took centuries to build and remain one of the world's greatest marvels. While other magnificent structures were built and later wasted away, the pyramid remains strong and magnificent. How they were built is still somewhat of a mystery. Similarly, the character of a leader is also built with some degree of mystery. Character, like the pyramid, is constructed layer by layer over time without hardly being noticed. So it is with the exceptional leader....the *Alpha!*

As new leaders, character must be your hallmark. It takes time to build and its foundation must become so deeply rooted that regardless of turbulence in the organization, changes in the environment, or volatility in the markets, character must be like the pyramids...*stable and unshaken!* Leaders understand that their success in any endeavor will largely depend on their character, not their persuasiveness nor charisma. Before entering into a position of authority, determine to what degree of character you project to those who interact with you. This process is not limited to those who are subordinate, but also those senior and external. People may never deal with you more than a few times, but they can attest to your character based on the image that is consistently projected. Like the pyramid, character is the foundation of how a new leader is perceived. Keep your foundation solid.

To be seen as a person with good character, especially a new leader, you must be transparent. It isn't enough for others to see you, they need to see through you. From this perspective, they gauge their level of respect and admiration of you. When they recognize that you have their interest as a priority and not your own personal agenda, you provide a model for them to emulate. This fosters a level of trust that compels them to follow you and achieve higher aspirations because you demonstrate the epitome of leadership.

New leaders must ask themselves, "Who am I and what do I believe?" Are you willing to sacrifice your character to make the next promotion or increase your salary? What are you doing in secret that could compromise your character if it were ever exposed? Character is the same as integrity. This refers to the concepts of being pure in intent, word, meaning, and action. Character protects your words because if your character is solid and you possess integrity, they can trust what you say. Understanding that integrity is the principle that surrounds character, it enables the leader to embrace these concepts.

There is an old saying, "If you want to test a man's character, give him power". Another says, "Power corrupts". While these quotes are true, they are only true in part. A true Alpha does not seek to have power. In fact, they do not even seek to lead. Leadership and power are bestowed on them by those who are following. The characteristic action of the Alpha is to serve first.

Speaker, author, and consultant, Alan Weiss said, "Power does not corrupt. Powerlessness corrupts." While eloquently stated, one could say that power does not corrupt, rather It actually reveals corruption. Power reveals the true character of the person within. It cannot change you, but it will expose you.

Provoking Question:

Can your pyramid be shaken by power? Better yet, can it be bought?

Clear Your Mind of Can't

"The only thing that can grow is the thing you give energy to" - **Ralph Waldo Emerson**

Doubt is the precursor of ineffectiveness. Some new leaders look at the position they are about to assume with excitement and great anticipation. That is, until they see all the nuances that the position calls for. The initial reaction can be overwhelming and this is where the doubt trickles in. The new leader must recognize that their belief system is infectious *(more on this later)*. Even the Alpha recognizes that they have limitations, but they do not allow those limitations to hinder their progression nor that of their team's development. Alphas do not allow "can't" to enter their mind nor permit it to extend into their vocabulary. They will either say, "No" or ask, "What are the alternatives?"

Clearing your mind of "Can't" is a process that must be adopted and applied into the psyche of new leaders especially those who have never been in leadership. Managers say, "We can't". Leaders say, "How can we?" When the idea of "Can't" is introduced, the mind does not need to think any further because the decision is already made. This is not the thinking of exceptional leadership. "How can we?", invites a higher level of consciousness that activates limitless possibilities. "Can't" leads to failure while "How" leads to fortune. What leaders believe is projected onto those around them. That projection is transformed into buy-in from others as long as the passion of the leader is present. True leaders take others into the unknown. There is a saying. "Can't never could because can't never tried." Leaders will never excel if they never try.

True leadership doesn't bask in the questions of "Why", but in the challenges of, "Why not". While most average leaders see obstacles, exceptional leaders see opportunities. New leaders must take caution when making decisions of what does and does not happen. Simply jumping off the cliff because a senior says do it is foolishness. "Can't" to an Alpha simply means there are other alternatives to achieve the same result. Regardless of the circumstances, true leaders find a way. If they do not have the resources, they will find someone who does. *The Laws of Success* author, Napoleon Hill said, "You can do it if you believe you can."

Provoking Question:

Is "Can't" in your vocabulary?

Feel the Heat

"People don't change when they see the light, they change when they feel the heat." – **George C. Fraser**

Seldom do leaders emerge through choice. They are usually born though crisis or problems. When we look at history for great leaders, we often find situations where one or more leaders evolved as a result of it. Examples such as Moses during Israel's slavery, Mahatma Ghandi, during the oppression of his people under British rule, Nelson Mandela, during apartheid, and Martin Luther King Jr., during the civil rights movement. Crisis is when a true leader arrives to deal with the matter or to lead others through it. As mentioned, leaders first seek to serve others. They chose to forget the fire and feel the heat.

New leaders do not truly understand the next level until their own beliefs are tested. This is the point where they must feel the heat of problems, external influences, decision making, and resistance to change. True leadership, especially for new leaders, will always be tested for authenticity. New leaders must evaluate their beliefs and determine if they are willing to stand alone and be subjected to ridicule rather than compromise principles.

Research leaders of the current era and see what

conditions allowed them to rise. You may notice they were dealing with some form of opposition. Whether it is in the workplace, in the place of worship, or in the home, leaders are dealing with problems that humanity needs a resolution to. Simply going to work, directing or delegating others, having a huge salary, big office with an extravagant title does not make you a leader. Regardless of status, there is always a fire somewhere that is heating things up.

Some leaders want their organization to appear successful, and sometimes they can do the wrong thing just to make their company look good to others. CEOs of organizations like WorldCom and Enron experience the heat when the integrity of their organization was scrutinized because of self-indulgence and personal weakness. When they were called into question regarding ethical practices, this is when they felt the heat of scandal. Sometimes feeling the heat of turmoil is good for a leader's development if only to test their resilience regarding there adaptability or their will to stick to their principles.

New leaders must never seek to lead people in a way that establishes a dominant persona, but rather to share power and embrace the experiences and concerns they have to better understand their needs. Get deep into the trenches with them to feel the heat of deadlines, information gathering, product creation, innovative ideas, etc.

A leader must enter their team's world if they are ever going to lead them out of disorder. Understand their personalities; know about their experiences; what motivates them; what are their concerns or challenges; what do they value; what are their aspirations? The more you know about them, the better you can serve them and the more they will support your cause.

Provoking Question:

You may be willing to walk through the fire, but can you stand the heat?

CHAPTER 2

LEADERSHIP

"I am not afraid of an army of lions led by a sheep. I am afraid of an army of sheep lead by a lion"

– Alexander the Great

LEADERSHIP

Let's dismiss the idea that people work for the leader. In truth, leaders work for the people. I realize this is counterintuitive, but look at this point of view; as a leader, especially those who have just assumed the role of a leader, you delegate and direct instructions as necessary, but the people are the ones who give you that right or authority to do these things. Similar to the presidential elections, the people give the President the right to make policy, issue orders, and make decisions concerning them and their livelihood. That authority is given by *"the people"*, not taken by the leader. You are a servant to the people, but with a leadership authority. This is referred to as, *Servant Leadership.*

Leaders are able to inspire people to act. Those who are able to inspire give people a sense of purpose or belonging that has little to do with any external benefit, but for the realization of a cause that is greater than themselves. Though relatively few in number, leaders with a natural ability to inspire us come in many forms. They are found in both the public and private sectors. Regardless of where they exist, they all have a significant amount of influence in their industries. Here is the confusing part for most people: the greatest leaders are seen as the president, founder, CEO, or executive of a company, but in all truth, they are the only ones shown through media coverage. They are usually the person that is behind the scene who is making things happen.

Leadership determines everything because it is about movement and change. It is impossible to be a leader and not change things. Leaders step beyond boundaries and initiate creativity. As mentioned before, leadership moves people from the known circumstance to the unknown. This unknown area is known as vision. Sometimes being a leader, especially an Alpha, will lead you into discomfort because some changes will make the organization uncomfortable. Whenever a leader stops moving forward, they become just a manager because managers maintain things as they are. Leaders look to transform things such as projects, products, systems, services, circumstances, environments, and yes, even people.

Although we all can become excellent leaders, we cannot all become exceptional unless we know what an exceptional leader is and understand its true nature. It is often impossible to fully define the concept of an exceptional leader, or as I like to call it, the "Alpha" because of its complexity. Being exceptional consist of a multitude of diverse qualities, qualifications, components, skills, and various other elements. It is however, founded in the mindset and development of self. True leadership is not technique, it is attitude of the mind. To go even deeper, true leadership is not just the act of the aforementioned components, it is the result of them.

To grasp these concepts, it is necessary to formulate a foundation to build upon. The following sections will address some areas dealing with becoming a new leader in route to becoming an Alpha and adopting the Alpha attitude:

THE CONCEPTS

The Lynch Pin

"A great person attracts great people and knows how to hold them together." – **Johann Wolfgang Von Goethe**

True leadership is not about directing or controlling others, but about self-discovery. Leaders understand who they are and what their special gifts are. When assuming a new leadership role, it is natural for them to feel a sense of anxiety with the new level of responsibilities that come along with the position. New leaders understand that groups and organizations are always unique in culture and have their own personality. Still, all exceptional leaders share three common areas: to serve, to leave the world better than they found it, and to empower others. With this understanding, the new leader must realize that cultivating these dynamics are paramount, but self-discovery as the leader is the lynch pin for greatness.

Alphas give others a sense of meaning because they find purpose in their own lives which produces an awareness of their identity *(More on this later)*. This discovery provides a level of self-worth and value in the leader's mind. When a leader has discovered who they truly are, then confidence in their ability awakens. This can become a problem for new leaders because all too often there is an acquaintance between leadership and power. Such relation, while true in a practical sense, is merely an illusion.

Arrival to the leadership position provides more

obstacles than what is generally realized. People who assume new leadership roles can often be misled into believing that because they have a leadership position, they automatically have leadership power. Nothing could be further from the truth. The new leader tends to only see *POWER*. This is how the leadership mindset becomes corrupt. There is an old adage that says, "Seeing is useless if the mind is blind."

Who an average leader sees in the mirror with their eyes is a facade. It is just a physical form to present in the workplace and to the world. Simply looking like the stereotypical leaders doesn't make you one. Who the leader is in their subconscious mind is truth. That truth will project itself in words and actions. When the discovery of true-self is aligned with thought, word, and action and focused on the betterment of humanity... the Alpha is born. They do not confuse their leadership position with their leadership disposition.

Let's be clear so there is no misunderstanding. Leadership is not something you DO, it is something you ARE. Each person, regardless of what occupation or position has leadership within them. Workers, managers, even CEO's are so busy *"doing"* that they never start *"being."* It is when we become our true selves, our natural leadership emerges. To become an exceptional leader, the Alpha, you must first believe that you are one. Remember, being an Alpha is not a destiny, but a discovery. This discovery is the lynch pin of truly becoming an Alpha.

Provoking Question:

Are you a lynch pin in your organization?

The "Connection" Infection

"Before you are a leader, success is about growing yourself. When you are a leader, success is about growing others." **– Jack Welch**

Leadership is first personal, then it is public. Alphas first understand themselves, then they understand others. The main reason that most leaders fail, especially new ones, is because they fail to recognize that human relationship is the engine that powers leadership. Regardless of what others may believe, we must establish relationships for leadership to thrive. Organizations respect leaders who value the relationships they build with colleagues, customers, and executives because it generates productivity, performance, and harmony.

When leaders understand the components of the organization's teams and their needs, they attract cooperation... *They connect*. This process is what I call the "Connection" infection. To better emphasize this concept, here is an excerpt from the book, *People Follow* You by Jeb Blount, *"The best leaders are the best relationship builders. These leaders understand that success as a leader is directly and entirely related to the quality of relationships they build and sustain with the people they lead."*

To be clear in understanding this connection process, new leaders who desire to become Alphas must know that your people are more important than you. Let me say that again, "Your people are more important than you." Saying you are a manager, director, or some other fancy title does not make you a leader. It only gives you a degree of authority over others. The legacy of leadership comes when you, as the leader, are no longer necessary.

What does this mean, *No longer necessary?* By this I mean you have developed your team to become as competent or influential to an extent that your presence is no longer required to lead them. You have, therefore, created the next group of leaders. This is why Alphas never hold too tightly to a position they currently have. If you are always needed to instruct others under your charge, this is evidence that you are not yet an Alpha. True leaders develop others to become leaders. They do not maintain followers. Once a new leader has assumed a position, they should automatically and immediately be looking for their replacement. This is where connection comes into play and mentorship is formed.

New leaders must adopt a practice of really knowing and understanding those they work with and work for. This process is ongoing and provides an in-depth view into the abilities and mentality of others. Alphas identify who is best suited as a replacement and where others need to be developed and groomed for leadership. Titles do not make you a leader, service does. Everyone is made to lead, but they must go through a process to become the leader. As a new leader, it becomes necessary to groom your replacement quickly because the better a leader you become, the less titles you need.

So, you ask, "How do I, as a new leader connect with people so it becomes infectious?" Who you are at the core will inevitably appear despite any façade you may present. Therefore, you must first know who you are as a person to determine what about you should be adjusted in order to create the "Connection" infection.

Here are some recommendations:

- **Assess your own personality and how you react to others.** Understand your leadership style and its challenges. Before a leader can understand others, they must first understand themselves. Avoid prejudging people based on limited knowledge or experience. Not everyone receives instructions in the same way, and they do not connect in the same manner.

- **Treat everyone equally and respectfully.** People wish to be accepted and appreciated for who they are and what they bring intellectually. Remain professional and never gossip or joke about others. When you devalue others, you devalue your credibility and leadership.
- **Be approachable.** Nothing repels others more than when they know you are avoiding them or being distant. As a new leader, you must be approachable. To develop and learn from people, you must engage them. You cannot develop or change what you avoid.
- **Develop others.** A key function of a new leader is to identify and connect with their team to determine the level of competency of each individual and what additional training they require to be more efficient. Everyone grows independently; therefore, they do not learn in the same way or at the same speed. Leadership connection builds rapport and allows information to be transferred between the leader and the team. This is referred to as coaching and mentoring. Remember, you are

creating new leaders, not just efficient workers.

- **Recognize and acknowledge the talents of others.** Often, recognition pays higher dividends for a leader's connection with people rather than money. Simply knowing that the leader sees the work of the employee and demonstrates appreciation by *public* recognition fosters a greater level of commitment from the employee/future leader.
- **Help others to fit in.** Everyone, regardless of personality or environment, wishes to fit in at some level. Leaders must create cultural norms that keeps everyone engaged and focused on positive interactions and high performance. Employees who feel they don't fit in become distant, ineffective, and disingenuous. Employees don't leave companies, they leave leaders. Show them how to fit in so their true talent can stand out.
- **Listen more, talk less.** This is an important, if not the most important, area of concern from people in the workplace about leaders. It is difficult to learn anything if you are always talking. The easiest way to connect is to ask probing questions and listen to understand

rather than to make a response. People are more apt to connect with you faster when they know you care about what they say. The more you listen, the more you learn. New leaders must create a habit of sincerely listening because the listening process is not only a physical one for followers, but an emotional one.

- **Communicate a clear vision of the future.** The leader is responsible for providing clear communication to the team about what direction they are going and why. If they don't know where they are moving toward and why, then they do not have a clear picture of their role nor where to channel their focus and energy. It is not enough to know, *Where; but also, to know Why.*

- **Be honest and trustworthy.** Nothing can devalue a leader faster than being known as dishonest and untrustworthy. Trust is the currency of leadership and the source of character. Without the pillar of trust, regardless of what power you wield, you can NEVER hope to be positively effective nor gain the connection to your organization.

- **Be consistent**. This is a trust building aspect of leadership. This action of consistency develops a perception of how a leader is viewed in daily habits. When others know what to expect from you in a given situation, it is easier for them to adapt to your style. Character is displayed in public, but tested in secret. Are you the same leader when no one else in watching?

Abraham Lincoln said, *"If you would win a man to your cause, first convince him you are his sincere friend."* A leader's ability to connect with others is not only about building trusting friendships, but also about influencing behavior. If a new leader wants to gain the cooperation and connection with others, they must make them feel important and they are vital to a greater cause. Strong working relationships are indicators of a healthy and effective organization. What are some of the benefits that leaders gain from others as a result of positive connection with the organization? Here are a few:

- Improved Productivity
- Improved attitudes
- Improved quality
- Reduced turnover
- Higher morale
- Increased safety

- Effective communication

Connecting with people as a new leader is like looking at the smooth surface of a lake and seeing an object moving slowly, but stealthily across. On the surface, you know something is happening, but to get a clearer picture, you must go beneath it to see what lurks.

New leaders must look below the surface to discover the truth of what is swimming in the heart and mind of others. When you reach the core of a person or group and they know you care about what is hidden within them, you have created a link. This is the "connection" infection.

Provoking Question:

How infectious is your connection?

Power through Empowering

"When you give people power, you see their true character. When you give them empowerment, you see their true courage." – **Terry T. Budget**

The transition to Alpha leadership from management or employee level is not the easiest task for most. To move to a leadership position and be effective, you must change your thinking to a leadership mindset. To become an effective leader transitioning into an Alpha, you must understand who you are versus who you want to be. You must discover the real you. As mentioned in, "Pyramid of Character," *"If you want to know a man's character, give him power."* When discovering the real you, you uncover your true worth, personal value, and power. However, true power comes from empowering others.

Your people are more important than you. Average leaders look for ways to improve performance for themselves and for those they work with while exceptional leaders, the Alphas, train others to maximize their potential and include them in leadership decisions. This process of empowerment invites commitment to a cause or an objective. Others must feel they are significant to a situation and the goal of a leader is not to manipulate with coercion, but to inspire through encouragement.

Great leaders understand that conflict amongst members do arise and in some cases, can actually be productive to lead teams to better outcomes. Exceptional leaders who invite conflict view differences of opinions as healthy and mediate the conflicts to consider all angles and possibilities to any situation. Their goal is to incorporate different perspectives within the team to allow them to see that everyone is important and has valuable contributions.

Although there can be some distractions within the group, the respected leader empowers each one to consider the other's point of view and creates methods to resolve the matters where both leave with a sense of personal satisfaction.

First, understand the needs of those who follow you. It is impossible to guide others to the next level until you know where they currently are. Leaders do not motivate followers to go to the next phase of greatness, but they search for the wants and needs that motivate them. Then, they empower them based on those motivations.

Leaders empower followers through personal accountability. Taking responsibility for their own actions gives individuals and teams the autonomy to act accordingly, but within specified boundaries of authority. This method encompasses ideas, engagements, actions, and goals just to name a few. Additionally, they empower others to stretch their imagination, knowledge, and abilities past what is comfortable and challenges them to expand them. Most people rise to the challenge when they are inspired or given encouragement to grow. Author, speaker, and leadership expert, John Maxwell said, "Leaders may impress others when they succeed, but they impact others when their followers succeed."

Consider legendary basketball player, Michael Jordan. He was a great example of a leader in the sports world from 1984-2002. If you review his career, you will discover that between 1984-1990, the Chicago Bulls failed to make it to the NBA Finals because of a lack of leadership from their star player. Regardless of how exceptional his ability was, he could not win without his team. Most games where he scored 30 or more points, the Bulls lost. It is not enough to have great skills if you never empower others to elevate themselves. True leaders know that they cannot do everything alone; they need a cohesive team.

From 1991-1993 and 1996-1998, you will discover that he incorporated the rest of his team into the plays and took over the game only when his exceptional ability was needed. When the team felt valued and trusted by their leader, they felt empowered; and as a result, they started winning championships. He became a symbol of excellence through disciplined activities. To become legendary, he did what other players would not do. After each game, he remained on the court to practice in areas where he knew his skills were weakest, and he encouraged the team to do the same. His discipline empowered and inspired his team as well as the world to believe they could *be like Mike!*

Leaders also empower others to learn from their mistakes. Alphas are especially good at acknowledging their mistakes, assessing them, fixing them, and moving forward. Although they do not forget the mistake, they also do not relive it. They empower others to follow their examples. It is not beneficial to continually dwell on old issues because it hinders progression. It is only a problem when a person fails to learn from it. An old adage is, "Forget the blame, fix the problem." Learn, don't linger.

To measure the success of a leader, look at the success of those who follow them. Leaders do all they can to set others up for success. You can tell the effectiveness of a leader by the effectiveness of their team. When one wins, they all win. Leaders empower each other to build and never complain about who did what or who gets the credit. They instill self-satisfaction in knowing they achieved a goal, but they make every effort to ensure contributors are recognized publicly. Below are some questions exceptional leaders should have their team ask themselves to help them discover their leadership capabilities:

- What is missing that I can fix?
- What should be done that only I can do?
- What significant difference can I make to improve team performance?
- How can I bring more value with what I have?
- Who can I help to be better?

Provoking Question:

As a new leader, what are you doing to empower your team to greatness?

You Are Always on Stage

"Become the kind of leader people would follow voluntarily, even if you had no title or position."
– Brian Tracy

When you attain the position of a leader, many followers or colleagues just see... *Position!* As a new leader, you must be prepared to mentally establish yourself as a leader through word and deed. No matter where you are, whether in the office or away, everyone sees you: you are always on stage. How others perceive you on a daily basis impacts their reactions. From your facial expressions to the stride of your walk, from the tone of your voice to your silence, and from what you do to what you don't do will determine the actions others take. Teams always want to know they are on the same page with the leader. When you change the page, you change the stage!

Regardless of the level of leadership you ascend, others will alter how they deal with you contingent upon your character and level of responsibility. How a leader is perceived will be based on their actions because they are always being watched. Never forget that regardless of your position or location, someone is always watching you. Do not be naïve to think that everyone wants you to succeed. In fact, the closest colleague to a new leader can be the very person watching for your weakness to be exploited. Be mindful who you share the stage with.

Promote your strengths, but surround yourself with those who are strong in areas that you are weak. Former US President Ronald Reagan was asked why he was so successful at being the President. He responded, "... because I staff my weakness." Keep strong people around you so when you are on stage, you have a strong supporting cast.

A fatal flaw of many new leaders and, for that matter, more experienced ones, is the belief of what they do outside the office is none of anyone's business. This thinking is absurd. When you are a leader, everything you do is everyone's business. Everyone around you watches your performance to determine what you will do or how you will respond in a given circumstance or situation. Your performance is a testament of your character and attitude. This is the plumb line of your leadership.

How should you perform when you are on stage?

Here are some recommendations:

- **Smile** - Nothing is more appealing or inviting than a leader who smiles. This simple action promotes approachability from others. This also acts as an attitude initiator and affects the climate of the day.
- **Look Professional** - When at work or in social gatherings, people are consciously aware about the appearance of others around them. As a new leader, never appear as a slouch because how you present yourself to others is a mental presumption of who you are or how you will perform.
- **Be courteous and assertive** - When engaging others, courtesy and respect is paramount. Leaders get things done, but are never so arrogant or aggressive that it impedes the accomplishment of the desired outcome.
- **Keep your hands clean** - What is done in the dark will ultimately come to light. Never place your integrity into question. Ensure what you say and what you do are in alignment. Do the right thing even when no one is looking.
- **Team First** - Never place your personal ambitions above that of the team success. Your goal as a new leader is to teach and

mentor others to win. In short, you must become so great of a leader to your team that you become obsolete. Remember, they not only watch your actions in their presence, but also your actions when you are away.

Provoking Question:

Are you the same person when the curtain is closed?

The Diversity Effect

"There are two ways of spreading light; to be the candle or the mirror that reflects it." – **Edith Wharton**

Only a fool believes they are self-made. Any person who has ever had major success has always had a team to support them. I gave the example in the previous section regarding Michael Jordan's inability to win championships without trusting in his team. The same holds true with individuals who have emerged into leadership. Leadership determines the destination of those that follow. Although we are all from diverse groups with independent personalities, we can all work together to attain the same goals. The goals are not attained without good leadership and team efforts. Trust must be mutual even when others have different beliefs.

Diversity and inclusion is one of the biggest challenges organizations face. We lead or are led by people who do not look like us. The face of America and the rest of the world is changing to reflect the diversity of other cultures especially in positions of leadership responsibility. As new leaders, the need to adopt different perspectives and include new ideas as a critical component of the leadership development process is paramount.

One of the most prolific organizations that has evolved to become both diverse and inclusive is the United States military. Although it took many years to achieve this level of acceptance, it is here. Leaders, even at the highest echelons of government have incorporated individuals from varying backgrounds. Since the Civil Rights Act of 1964 to present day, organizations have placed immense value on the need to integrate other ethnic groups into areas of leadership.

One of the challenges new leaders in corporate companies have, especially on an executive level, is developing a solid base for diverse leadership talent at those levels. Some organizations have achieved success in this endeavor, but to increase the percentage in other corporations takes the emphasis, influence, and collaboration of the entire company's leadership. Current leaders must recognize that each person can bring value and influence in the workplace based on their diverse characteristics and intellect. True leadership should not support visions or processes that give validation to social or corporate injustice. This is especially true with diversity.

Globalization and demographic changes are significant contributing factors that direct the change of perceptions in favor of diversity. New leaders must strive to effectively emphasize cross-cultural understanding to improve relations resulting in diligent effectiveness across borders. Due to the increase of global business, team effectiveness and inclusion of other cultures should be the central focal point of any organization. True leaders deliver others from the inhibitors of professional and social environments especially within diverse groups.

So how do you as a new leader ensure the team is not just diverse, but inclusive? Here are some recommendations:

- **Vision supporting a diverse organization** - Leaders must create a short and long-range culture that encourages and supports a workforce involving different ethnic and cultural groups, races, and ages at multiple levels of the organization. Expression of this view can be demonstrated through models or practices that reinforce this dynamic.
- **Willingness to change mindsets** - It is the leader's behavior and mindset that determines the validity of the acceptance of cultural diversity. Whatever attitude or leadership style is demonstrated regarding diverse teams is what is considered acceptable in the mind of others.

- **Mentoring diverse teams** - New leaders of diverse teams must assume an active role in the placement and positioning of these groups by creating opportunities for them to express and implement their individual skills or abilities. Alphas encourage growth in others regardless of backgrounds.
- **Diversity knowledge and awareness** - Understanding the language differences and customs of a particular culture enables new leaders to include those differences in the cohesion of the team. Cultural awareness is pivotal to team success. When there is awareness and acceptance, there is cooperation.
- **Culture diversity programs** - Leaders can introduce and implement programs that promote the hiring, inclusion, and career advancement of these groups to ensure respect and acceptance in the organization and aid in establishing it as an organizational norm.

Today, effective leaders recognize that diversity sparks innovation and creativity, spurs growth, and leads to better decision making. Regardless of culture or ethnic group, integration of diverse groups creates a greater competitive advantage. Employees with global experience and cultural sensitivity are in high demand because many organizations are conducting business internationally. To compete in a diverse world as a new leader, it is necessary to include a diverse demographic.

There are many advantages to an organization by incorporating some of the above recommendations. They are:

- Improved moral
- Better business image
- Employee value
- Greater organizational learning
- Stronger team performance
- Attracting and retaining talent
- Better business relationships
- Openness to new ideas, models, and initiatives

Provoking Question:

As a leader, are you a champion of diversity? How do you respond to diversity and inclusion in your organization?

You Can't Dunk on Me

"A great leader's courage to fulfill his vision comes from passion, not position." – **John Maxwell**

Who doesn't enjoy sports? One of my favorite sports is basketball. One of the most embarrassing situations, if not the most embarrassing, is to have another player dunk on you. I've seen it many times and I jump out of my seat each time it happens. However, to get to the goal to perform the dunk, the player has to get past the defender. I call them defensive barriers. Before games, average players tell superstars, "You're good, but you can't dunk on me."

New leaders assume new responsibilities as they take on different roles. Often, they will encounter resistance from seniors or junior managers and employees that tend to challenge their direction. These are considered as organizational barriers. Sometimes, these barriers are introduced due to the actions of the leaders themselves. Defensive barriers grow subtly and often without notice. The object is to identify them and create a plan of how to break them down to produce innovation, productivity, and creativity. According to Frances Hesselbein, international speaker and seminar leader on leadership, some of these barriers are self-imposed barriers and others are institutional barriers. We will choose a relevant designation to better illustrate the concept. They are:

"One-on-One" Barriers

- Lack of articulated, personal goals
- Misunderstanding of one's strengths and weaknesses
- Lack of business ethics (Personal and Professional)
- Lack of generosity
- Leading from the rear

Team Barriers

- Hierarchical structures that restrict people
- Cultures that encourage mediocracy
- Racism and Sexism
- No Mentorship
- Diversity

Considering all these barriers that prevent the new leader from getting to their goal, let's discuss some ways that we can get through them to complete the *dunk* and win the game of leadership. New leaders have the One-on-One barriers; but sometimes, you have to get past the whole team.

First, let's develop plays to deal with the one-on-one barriers and then deal with the team barriers to get to our goal or "complete the dunk":

Man-to-Man Defense:

- Personal goals should be written and available for reference to the new leader. Simply having an idea of them is ineffective. They should be clear enough for not only the leader to understand, but also the team. The game plays must be understood.
- Know where your strengths are. Build upon them and surround yourself with those who are strong in your areas of weakness (See: *You are Always on Stage*). Every team has a superstar.
- If you have no personal or professional ethics, you cannot be trusted. You become ineffective as a leader. Create a moral compass to guide you. Before doing things right, do the right thing first. Make the team success more important than your personal ambitions.
- Share ideas, respect, commitment, and empowerment with others. You will build a team of Alphas that exceed expectations. Leadership thrives by building relationships

and empowerment. Leaders succeed when they commit to the team.
- Average leaders inspire the team to follow them while Alphas inspire them to become leaders themselves. Teams should be able to win even when the leader is out of the game.

Zone Defense:

- Organizational structures tend to be very rigid and inflexible. New leaders must learn and encourage their teams to learn as much about other departments as possible. Increase your value by learning and understanding different positions, not just your own.
- Refine and master your skills. The more valuable you are to the team, the more maneuverability you have to grow. Mastery creates opportunities and opens the lane to the goal.
- Inability to accept other races and sexes is detrimental to the group objective. New leaders must huddle the team together and embrace everyone's ability. That is how games in leadership are won and corporate failures are broken down.
- Empower others to do their best and never give up. Give your knowledge and experience to

the team to make them better than they believe they can be. Encouragement builds strength and breaks down defenses.
- Diversity generates collaboration. Regardless of skill levels, one idea elicited from a different culture can change the leadership playbook and alter the outcome of the game. Get fresh ideas from your team to make innovative, game changing plays.

Regardless of the barriers that inhibit a leader or a team from becoming great, there are methods to combat these issues. The idea is to begin to identify them and initiate plans to preempt them from occurring or formulate practices that defend the organization when they happen. Trust your team to work the best plays that lead to the win. More so, trust your instincts. Remember, the point is to get to the goal.

Provoking Question:

How are you breaking down your barriers to reach the goal?

CHAPTER 3

PURPOSE

"Efforts and courage are not enough without purpose and direction." **– John F. Kennedy**

PURPOSE

There is an Alpha in everyone waiting to be released. To become an Alpha, you must return to your original purpose. There are two ways to discover the purpose that has been lurking inside of you. You can either learn it or you can experience it. As you commit to the process of becoming an exceptional leader, the Alpha, you will be able to (1) discover your true identity, (2) develop your gifts and talents, (3) leave your mark, and (4) inspire others to find their purpose within them.

New leaders must look within themselves and discover what is unique about them that makes them valuable. For new leaders, this process can seem confusing because they look at the position they have as the purpose of them being in the organization when in truth, what they are actually performing is a role or function. New leaders do not need a position, but a disposition. Position is external, what you *"do";* while disposition is internal, who you *"are"*. This idea refers to the temperament of the mind.

THE TEMPERAMENT

Why Me?

"A true leader's work is not a job or a career, but the very life he lives" **– Dr. Miles Munroe**

Each person has the capacity to lead. The question which challenges the thinking of organizations is, "Are leaders born or are they made?" The answer is… both! Identifying the reason why you are a leader is irrelevant if you do not believe you're one in the first place. There is something that only "YOU" are able to do and the intent is to discover what that purpose is and learn how to maximize it.

Unlike average leaders, Alphas do not focus on making a high income, but making a high impact. In his book, *The Leadership Handbook*, John Maxwell wrote, *"Millions saw the apple fall, only Newton asked why."* Leaders must discover how to make a difference in their team, in their organizations, and the world, but they must first discovery their *"Why."*

In the section, *Power through Empowering*, I gave the example of Michael Jordan and his abilities to empower his team to win. He found his gift, mastered it, and delivered it to the world. He found his purpose. Without purpose, life has no meaning. New leaders must discover what their gift is and master it. Whether it is in the organization or outside, leaders must discover their purpose and explore the boundaries of their uniqueness. Alphas recognized this and discovered it quickly in order to become influential.

You must believe that as an Alpha, you are a person of purpose with built in potential to fulfill it. Remember in Chapter 1, we discussed the idea of self-discovery. When you have the conviction of who your truly are, what your uniqueness is, and the potential to become it, you have discovered the Alpha within you. You have discovered your purpose. So, you ask, "Why me?" I respond, "Why not you?"

There is an old saying, "The greatest tragedy in life is not death. It is being alive and not knowing why." Organizations that range from small businesses to Fortune 1000 companies struggle with staying in tune with their reason for being. A great deal of individuals may state they exist to make money, but in truth, that is not their real purpose. Making money is simply a result of fulfilling their purpose. For a new leader assuming leadership responsibilities, whether it is a personal, professional or a spiritual quest, you must discover your *"WHY"* factor. Until you discover it and begin to master it, you will never become an Alpha.

Organizations look to leaders to provide them

with vision and purpose for their work. The problem is that organizations can only provide the purpose and vision for the company, but not for the group. Exceptional leaders inspire people to find vision and purpose for themselves. As mentioned in *The Lynch Pin*, leadership is about self-discovery and we only have to look within ourselves to find the hidden leader.

Purpose for life is an individual search and a personal unearthing. Leaders must understand that finding purpose for life and work is independently significant. Some find it in their job, while others find it in their work. There's a difference between the two. A job is what you are paid to do, but your work is what you are born to do. Your job is your skill in action while your work is your purpose being manifested.

Provoking Question:

Are you doing what you are paid for or what you are purposed for?

Create Your Value

"Knowledge is of no value unless you put it into practice"
– Anton Chekhov

If as a new leader you are trying to become successful, do not seek success. Seek to become a person of value. Success is expressed or demonstrated through the things you value. This usually comes in the form of goal accomplishment. The purpose of leadership is to groom followers to become leaders and help them fulfill their purpose through internal potential. Leaders who produce other leaders by helping them discover their purpose and potential have achieved both value from empowerment and success through transformation. Whether inside an organization or external to it, the same principle applies; become valuable and success will follow you.

So, how do you become valuable? A leader or the team becomes valuable when they discover the gift or ability they were meant to serve the community. Value is increased by acquisition, understanding, and application of knowledge and ability. Leaders look to grow and increase the value of their team by tapping into their knowledge and potential to create opportunities for that potential to be manifested. When people know what your knowledge and abilities are, they know what to come to you for.

According to author, Napoleon Hill, "Success is very largely a matter of adjusting one's life to be ever-varying and changing environments of life, in a spirit of harmony and poise." Comprehend that success is personal to each person and how they focus on it will determine if they achieve it. As mentioned in *Focus or Flatline,* leaders concentrate on the big picture without dismissing all the details. Those details give meaning to the big picture and create opportunity to venture into other areas for added value. New leaders must garner information from every possible source that leads to the realization of their purpose, the fulfillment of their vision, and increased value.

Consider Microsoft Corporation's mission statement, "Empower every person and organization on the planet to achieve more." Such a mission personifies the value not just of what they see in the products they sell, but also the people in the organization, to include, the consumer. Their reach is global and each time they create a new improvement to their product, the value added is increased by those improvements. New leaders should consider this model in terms of improving their own value and, as a result, added value to the organization. Companies generate value by the commitment of their people, not just on the products or services they render.

Value must first become an independent goal before it is a corporate one. Value is what is determined by the person while worth is what other people place on that perceived value. New leaders should evaluate themselves regularly to determine what value they currently have. The more value you have, the more others will pay for it. If others had to think about something that reminded them of you, what would it be? If others never thought about you that implies you have never made yourself valuable.

Find the one thing that you are skilled at and begin to master it. When you are a jack of all trades, you're a master of nothing. Knowing bits of many things diminishes your value to others. People, even organizations, will pay for specialized knowledge. The world is filled with general people; therefore, become so good in an area that you cannot be ignored. Create such value that people look for you because of it. The world pays for people to solve problems and the larger the problem a leader solves, the more valuable they become.

Provoking Question:

How are you making yourself, your team, and the organization more valuable?

Problems, Problems, Problems

"Every solution to every problem is simple. It's the distance between the two where the mystery lies"
– David Landy

New leaders and, for that matter, seasoned leaders work to solve problems. Whether or not they recognize this as a truth, it is at the heart of their function. Problems exist everywhere and each individual has some expertise, knowledge, or experience to solve them. The most valuable leader is the person who seeks out problems and offers solutions to them. The larger the problem a leader solves, the more valuable they become. To be more specific, the purpose of each leader or individual wanting to be a leader is growth, connection, and problem solving.

Consider the Wright brothers in their aim to create a flying machine. With this invention, the development of air travel solved the problem of timeliness for transportation. The problem of clean water availability was solved with the idea of filtering and bottling. Automated assembly solved the problem of expedited mass production. New leaders who assume these responsibilities must look past what already works and find ways to improve it or make it more efficient with less effort. Maintaining what already functions well only makes a person a manager. When a leader looks at productivity, they always seek alternative ways to make it better. New leaders should always look for problems to solve or preempt situations that could become problems.

New leaders must become intimately familiar with organizational concerns. Some of the concerns are globalization, innovation, governmental regulations, technology, and diversity. Let's examine these particular areas and their potential problems:

Globalization – This process deals with understanding foreign cultures and the ability to penetrate new markets with existing products. **Problem** - Gaining a better understanding of international markets and cultures through information gathering and examination. Trends and markets are always fluctuating and leaders must create strategies to stay updated with this influx.

Innovation - This is a method of generating new products or improving on old ones while still remaining true to the foundational service. **Problem** - How to become more innovative while still keeping a degree of dominance and significance in line with the original mission of the company.

Governmental Regulations – This deals with the laws

and guidelines that address specific industries about how business is conducted and, in some cases, with who they conduct business with. **Problem** - Understanding the impact and meaning of the regulations, its implications, and incorporating the knowledge needed to deal with them.

Technology – The ever changing world of information and improvements to technology create a vacuum for businesses to invest capital. Competitors are equally resilient to acquire new and more advanced technology to bring to the market before other companies. The wait game for advancements causes leaders risk on both sides. **Problem** – How to maintain flexibility during times of technological development and innovation while developing long-term strategies to implement them when they become available or when they change?

Diversity – This process, while increasing in recognition and implementation, is not without its challenges. It creates an environment where multiple cultures often disagree causing difficulty in running a business. However, it reduces single-mindedness in a world focused on globalization. **Problem** – Defining the relative meaning of diversity for the company and implementing plans to support the expansion of differing ideas and perspectives while ensuring cohesion within the groups.

Everyday problems among experienced and emerging leaders limits their ability to engage significant matters that arise in an organization's routine business dealings. Mid-level managers tend to become involved with one situation after the other depending on which executive sets it as their priority. Each day, another problem presents itself, but the new leaders objective is to prioritize and determine how and who is best suited to offer a viable solution. Alphas thrive on this because it presents them with new opportunities to experience the situation, cultivate new information, gather various points of view for a solution, and empowers others to be creative. Alphas see problems as growth development opportunities.

Provoking Question:

How do you see problems that come into your organization and who do you invite to solve them?

Close Your Eyes...Open Your Mind

"Make your vision so clear that your fears become irrelevant"- **Anonymous**

If you don't know where you're going, then how will you know when you get there? As leaders, we are so determined to deal with issues as they arise that we often forget to look at the bigger picture. We see things with our eyes just as they are. What some leaders do, even experienced ones, is fail to see the forest for the trees. They do not see how things could be and this is largely due to the impact of their current condition. New leaders must determine what the future should look like based on what legacy they wish to leave. They must know their destination for themselves, their team, and their organization. They must close their eyes and open their mind. We call this... *VISION!*

Vision dictates everything that happens in an organization and, for that matter, a leader's life. This does not mean that vision is solely for the organization. The new leader should have their own personal vision, as well as, support of the organization they work for or own themselves. Let's deal with the vision of the leader and its impact.

Everything you do should be motivated by your

vision because vision helps you identify yourself and your actions towards other people. When leaders open their mind to what they want to achieve, then possibilities present themselves.

Sight is the ability to see things as they are, while vision is the ability to see things as they could be. Identify what it is that you want to do so passionately that you would sacrifice almost anything for its realization. The following statement is an area that needs come clarification, so we must be careful when addressing it. Vision is not for the leader. Let me repeat that. "Vision is not for the leader." It only goes *through* the leader. Vision is ALWAYS, ALWAYS, ALWAYS for the betterment and service to others. If it only benefits the leader, it is not a vision. It is called ambition. More specifically, it is called *private* ambition.

As a new leader, or shall I say, an emerging Alpha, it becomes necessary to recognize the disciplines that vision impacts on their life and how it indirectly affects others. Vision determines your:

- **Friends** – In his book, *Looking Out for #1,* author, Robert Ringer wrote, "People will bother you until you no longer allow them to. Those who consistently exasperate you should be eliminated from your life, while those who display rational, positive qualities should be looked upon as welcomed additions." The people that a leader spends time with should be those who inspire and motivate them to pursue their vision and expand their thinking. Your association will determine your destination. Remember, some people can be toxic to your mind. How they influence you will determine how you, as a leader, influence others.

- **Books** – They are as poignant as people and just as influential. Remember that as a leader it is important to monitor what you feed your mind. The content material can sway how you perceive things and those around you, ultimately impacting your vision and perspectives. Books are the keys that unlock the prison of your mind.
- **Priorities** – Leaders ensure things are in order based upon importance. In his book, *Today Matters,* John Maxwell wrote, "Successful people make right decisions early and manage those decisions daily." When leaders marginalize their priorities, they minimized their vision. Make first things, first!

- **Use of Time** – Using time unproductively is not a regular function of an Alpha. Each minute of the day should have a purpose behind it. Regardless of intent, use of time in any given period must have a meaning focused on productivity. Even when physically relaxing, Alphas are always thinking and planning.
- **Attitude** - When an exceptional leader is passionate about their vision, it determines how they think. They are always mindful about their thinking process because it affects their ability to reach their goals and manifest their vision. They are aware that their attitude has an impact on others and continually keep it in check.
- **Hobbies** – People are free to choose the hobbies they want to spend time engaging in, but remember, a leader is aware of what environments those hobbies place them in. Let the things you do in your free time place you in environments that expand your vision and your networks. Alphas are constantly aware of what they do and who they do it with.

In his book, *The 48 Laws of Power,* Robert Green wrote this excerpt (Law 29),

"The ending is everything. Plan all the way to it, taking into account all the possible consequences, obstacles, and twists of fortune that might reverse your hard work and give the glory to others. By planning to the end, you will not be overwhelmed by circumstances and you will know when to stop. Gently guide fortune and help determine the future by thinking far ahead."

Leaders who have no vision disregard restraint and fail to plan effectively. Restraint refers to discipline or self-control. Without vision, actions taken can result in uncertainty. Without discipline, chaos reigns. New leaders must always maintain a level of control where the outcome of actions have a high degree of predictability to protect their vision. Vision for a person or organization should incorporate clarity and the improvement of something or others. New leaders must ensure that when they close their eyes and open their mind that their vision is not really *ambition* in disguise.

Provoking Question:

What do you see when you close your eyes?

CHAPTER 4

HONOR

"I would prefer to fail with honor than to win by cheating" – **Sophocles**

HONOR

A leader's honor is engraved in their actions and words. When leaders are called into question, their honor is immediately in jeopardy. Leaders who earned the right to express themselves in a form that is respectable and filled with integrity will rally others to their cause. Honor is the first cousin of integrity. The leader must always do the right thing and their actions will reflect that honor within. There was a time when a hand shake was enough to seal a deal placing a code of honor between men. Today, we deal in contracts and negotiations to ensure there is a legal premise to hold the other party accountable to their word.

Although the idea of having contracts between individuals or organizations has merit, the need for individuals who place their word as a standard of honor today fails in comparison to the standard that it once had. The fact that we now live in a litigious society, the value of honor has been diminished. When we call into question a person's word, we automatically diminish their honor. New leaders should consider establishing a personal leader's code that represents their moral values.

THE CODE

Way of the Warrior

"He who knows others is wise. He who knows himself is enlightened" – **Tao Te Ching**

In the Japanese culture, honor is a very serious matter. For example, the ancient Japanese Samurai were a group of warriors who fought for a specific cause, but maintained the way of the warrior. This was known as the *Bushido.* Although Bushido is an honor code, it was not written down until the 17th century, after Samurai had already been in existence for centuries. The sense of loyalty and honor was carried in the heart by the Samurai and they would fight to the death to protect it. Much like the Samurai, new leaders should adopt a code of moral ethics and sense of honor when related to their team and the organization.

In the movie, *The Last Samurai,* the character Captain Algren, played by Tom Cruise, was being trained by one of the senior Samurai. The other Samurai warriors, to include the son of their leader, Top Knot, watched the training. Top Knot observed the frustration of Captain Algren during the training and went over to him saying, "*… too many minds."* This referred to the fact that he was focused on everyone watching him train and not on the training itself. The lesson to new leaders is not to focus on what everyone else is watching regarding your actions, but more so on becoming a better version of yourself and improving others. Personal development and development of others brings its own honor.

Although never carried to the extreme of sacrificing one's own life, the dedication of a leader to the group and the organization runs a similar parallel that reflects their thinking. New and emerging leaders who wish to ascend to the thinking of an Alpha should consider portions of the Samurai ideal and look deep within their mind and character to discover the true warrior within. This ideal, as mentioned in *The Lynch Pin*, "Simply looking like the stereotypical leader doesn't make you one. Who the leader is in their subconscious mind is truth."

Leaders need the heart of a warrior because of the challenges they face. The conviction of staying in alignment with their vision can create problems in other areas of their lives, in addition to, that of their teams. This is especially true of a leader who is the owner of the company and deals with opposition of friends, family, and colleagues. A true leader does not give in when tribulations come, as they most certainly will. Average leaders who wish to be Alphas are committed to the essence of life and their noble values. They rise to a higher calling beyond themselves. Personal honor and the integrity of the team is the point of their sword.

Here are a few attributes that new and emerging leaders should embrace to become warriors (Alphas) of the future. Like the Samurai, leaders:

- **Don't Wait:** A leader doesn't wait for things to happen. They are initiators. They make things happen. They do not wait for other people to negotiate. They get it done. They do not wait for others to instruct. They literally begin instructing, but the first person they instruct is themselves.
- **Know Character Counts:** Like the Samurai, leaders must be very careful to protect their character and reputation because their name will go farther than they will. Additionally, they guard the reputation and character of their team.
- **Live in the Future:** They understand that not everyone thinks as they do, so they work in the present problem, but live in the future promise (vision). They walk ahead of the people, but never out of their sight.

Organizations can't follow their leader if they can't see them or know where they are going.
- **Know Their Values:** Leaders know what they value most and they continually share those values with others. Their goal is to be of uncompromised values and independent high morals.
- **Do Not Succeed Alone:** Leaders know that it takes a concerted effort of a team to have success. Leadership is a team sport so, they encourage and position others to win. When the team wins, everyone is a champion.
- **Live by Example:** Alphas are the model for others to emulate. What they do is an example of who they are and how they think. They lead from the front and demonstrate what they instruct others to do.

Provoking Question:

How will you earn and keep your honor?

Your Name Will Go Further Than You

"Reputation is character minus what you've been caught doing." – **Michael Lapoce**

Have you ever played the game of golf? It is a game of finesse, not power. When we look at all the great past and current players of the game, commentators mentioned something like how far a player may drive the ball from the tee to the fairway. Such names as, Phil Mickelson, Arnold Palmer, Jack Nicholas, and of course, Tiger Woods are discussed not because of how far they drove the golf ball, but how well they mastered the game. They became leaders of their gifts. As a result, their names are mentioned around the world, even in places they have never been. Their names will forever be revered and will go further than they ever will.

Leaders, especially those that are emerging to higher levels of responsibility must protect their image and reputation at all cost. For this reason, the attributes mentioned in the previous section are extremely vital. What does it say about a leader when they enter a room and the atmosphere changes to reflect their presence? Whether it is a positive or negative reaction, it is incumbent upon the leader to either embrace it or work to change it.

Even though people may not personally know you, they may *know of* you. Just like a golf ball, your name can travel far.

As individuals, we all have strengths and abilities that come to us more easily than others. It is not difficult to see in any group of leaders, that there are varying differences. Exceptional leaders find the spot where their talents and the organizational values blend. These leaders desire to be known for something that is significant and brings credit and value to them, their team, and the organization as a whole. They do not just strive to be efficient, but to be the authority in a specific area. Exceptional leaders want to be known as the go-to-person. Personal accolades are not the true goal, but they wish to be called upon because of the exceptional service they provide. These leaders understand that their name will go farther than they ever will.

Provoking Question:

What do people think of when your name is mentioned?

The Fish Rots from the Head

"A good leader leads from the front of the army, even though that might cost him his life. A bad leader hides behind the army, and that is what makes him lose the war." - **Unknown**

If you have ever been fishing and left a fish out of the barrel, you will see that over time the fish begins to rot. However, if you look closely, you will discover that the fish rots from the head and then infects the rest of the body. The same idea applies to corrupt leaders and their organizations. When people view the news that broadcast corporations that are experiencing problems, the focus is primarily on the leader or the leadership team.

The fraudulent ideas and actions of an organization start from its leaders. Regardless of who in the leadership platform initiates it, the corruption spreads like a virus and all members are directly or indirectly affected as a result. When the head is infected, the body ceases to function properly.

This impact is not exclusive to any one industry, but each organization must have leadership and how that leadership head functions, whether just or unjust, determines the capability of the organizations impact.

Below are some credentials a new leader should have to prevent organizations from deteriorating. They resonate deep in the leader's core and are personified through their actions. This list is not what just what leaders do, but who they should be. Exceptional leaders are:

- **Above Reproach:** The new leader should not have negativity following them because of past actions or deeds. Reputation is perceived truth; therefore, guard it with your life.
- **Temperate:** Those entering or currently in leadership must always be in control of their actions and words. This is an area of self-discipline. You must be very slow to anger and quick to resolve situations peacefully.
- **Respectable:** Respect comes from consistency of principles. Exceptional leaders do not change their standards or convictions. If a leader is not respected, they cannot inspire others or acquire allegiance.
- **Hospitable:** Be kind and take the time to spend with people. Talk to and listen to others with sincerity. People tend to avoid leaders when they are difficult to approach or get along with.

- **Able to Teach:** A new leader must be able to effectively communicate their ideas and thoughts. Without effective communication, there is a breakdown in understanding.
- **Not Negatively Impaired:** A leader cannot be involved in things or consume things that negatively affect their decision-making abilities. This includes substances or groups that threaten a productive culture because others well-being can depend on your decisions.
- **Not Money Driven:** Leaders seek to serve others first and transform others into successful leaders. Money is a by-product of service, not the foundation of it. The more people you serve, the more money you make. To Alphas, serving people is primary; money is secondary.

The German Regime of the 1940's was a military powerhouse. During its reign of power, their leader, or shall we say, dictator, seized power through fascist policies and the propaganda of creating a supreme master race. Despite Hitler's efforts to attack the Soviet Union and declare war on the United States, his army fell to the superior might of the aforementioned super power. Leadership is about inspiration, not manipulation.

When a leader uses manipulation to sway the cooperation of others, it disavows the honor of a leader. As a result, the entire corporate structure decays. When reviewing the above list, it becomes clear where some credentials were not present, which ultimately resulted in the leader's demise. Remember, the fish rots from the head!

Provoking Question:

How do your actions affect the body of your organization?

Walk Hard or Go Home

"The supreme quality for leadership is unquestionably integrity. Without it, no real success is possible, no matter whether it is on a section gang, a football field, in an army, or in an office." **– Dwight D. Eisenhower**

When a new leader wants to succeed and have their team succeed, they must put certain practices in place to keep their honor intact. Understanding that integrity will determine the outcome, new leaders should coach their team about the need to maintain it at all costs. If leaders have no honor, they become a figurehead with minimal to no influence. From the perspective of the rest of the organization, the new leader should either correct it or resign. In other words, *walk hard or go home*.

Many leaders dream big, but for some reason they lose sight of it and those that follow them tend to do the same. Sometimes to be a successful leader, you do not need to add more things to your list of goals or accumulate more knowledge, but remove some of the negative programing learned during the ascension to leadership. Some things that a leader should relinquish are:

- **Short-Term Mindset:** This mindset only creates short-term gratification and has the potential to place honor at risk. When a leader only has a short-term mindset, those they try to develop as leaders tend to dwindle because they are only learning short-term habits. **Solution:** Create a long-term mindset with a clear vision that is achieved through active daily habits. These daily habits accumulate in the acquisition of the long-range vision. Become accountable to someone to ensure your vision remains on track. They become your honor auditor.

- **Playing it Safe:** Leaders that never risk putting it all on the line, never reap the big rewards. Sometimes that means putting your honor or reputation on the line for something you believe in. **Solution:** When you take full ownership of your decisions and take action, others see the commitment you have and decide in their own mind if they will rally with you. A leader with honor is willing to risk standing alone. Walk hard or go home is their motto!

- **Excuses:** This is what separates average leaders from Alphas. Alphas find ways to get things done through creative thinking or acceptable alternatives; however, average leaders look at the obvious methods of doing things. When they don't meet the requirements, excuses of why they can't do it seem to arise. **Solution:** Connect with others who have a creative mindset and ask questions on how something can be done. Network with out-of-the-box thinkers who can introduce new perspectives. If you lack resources, then improve your resourcefulness. Get with the right people and resources will appear.

- **Likeability:** Weak leaders attempt to please everyone. They will sacrifice their moral convictions for the sake of others acceptance. They're willing to sacrifice their honor and their personal truth for approval. **Solution:** People who dislike you will begin to hate you when you maintain your honor despite ridicule; however, they must respect your conviction. Those that do like you will begin to love you for the same reason. Your character is a testament of your honor.

- **Negative People:** As mentioned in previous chapters, people can be toxic to your mind. They can drive you to a point where they push you to jeopardize your integrity. When you spend enough time with them you tend to become like them. **Solution:** Stop spending major time with minor people. The late author and speaker, Jim Rohn said, *"You are the average of the five people you spend your time with."* Identify and learn from the leaders in your circle who will never position you to jeopardize your honor or character.

Provoking Question:

As a leader, are you willing to stand alone to protect your honor?

CHAPTER 5

ACUMEN

"Material wealth does not last forever, but that which probably lasts forever is the wealth of intelligence and creativity"

– Michael Bassey Johnson

ACUMEN

Alphas understand that good and quick decision making can mean the difference between success and failure. In *Leaders Ought to Know,* author, Phillip Van Hooser writes, *"If leaders are willing to do only that which has been proven, assured, or commonplace, then they've already failed in their practical role as a leader."* Alphas take calculated risks and understand that playing it safe doesn't get it done. Their calculations are meticulous and they want to know details in efforts to make informed decisions. New leaders are faced with this similar situation as they manage the daily operational activities which are the components of the larger goal. They must understand that taking risks is not foolish, but not managing risk is.

Leaders with a high business acumen are those who think past what is currently happening and envision an environment as it could be. These are the Alphas of the business world. They are always aware of the level of risk involved and consider all potential outcomes. Even when they don't have all the details of a vision for bettering humanity, an existing product or service, or simply a process, they prepare themselves to charge forward even in the midst of opposition. New leaders should embrace the concept of stratospheric thinking as mentioned in Chapter 1.

THE MIND

Arm Yourself for Battle

"Act like a man of thought. Think like a man of action" –
Thomas Mann

Thinking about the core intention of the company a new leader owns or works for is essential. Therefore, it becomes crucial for them to consider the expectations of their stakeholders. Decisions made by leaders often create an environment of change. Change often meets resistance when others do not fully understand the direction or have become complacent with the usual way of doing things. New leaders are faced with the probability of change happening at any given moment; therefore, they must recognize any situations presented will test their acumen.

Over the past several years, the need for business acumen as an important competency has become the focal point of most CEO's. It is considered one of the top 10 critical areas of concern. Considering the irregularity of today's global economy, organizations are looking for leaders, managers, and employees, who can directly contribute to the achievement of their goals and objectives by making the right business decisions. When a leader goes into action and faces opposition, they must be armed with as much knowledge as those they face.

Regardless of position in an organization, every leader needs the skills and tools to think more like an owner of the business and to understand and execute business strategy while being able to measure the effectiveness of their strategy and performance. Acumen can be a brutal process especially when a leader struggles to garner buy-in from others. As a leader, you must arm yourself for battle.

A great business acumen presents everyone with all the information and tools they need to see and understand situations. Making good and informed decisions becomes a critical component to a leader's success especially when driving down costs and improving quality and customer focus. Leaders must be equipped to handle any adversity because their decisions affect other people within the organization and their alliances with external vendors. Some of them are not ready for battle and fail because:

- The leader's decisions may be good, but it is not fully developed or communicated to others.
- Organizational systems are not aligned with the change.
- Those being asked to change are not involved in the decision-making process.
- People are not held accountable for implementation of the decision.
- Employee's concerns about the decisions are not addressed.

Tomorrow's leaders must acquire vast amounts of knowledge and surround themselves with those who possess the knowledge they lack. Their acumen regarding how to lead and what is necessary to remain ready for battle in a corporate sense is important because the ability to anticipate and envision the future, maintain flexibility, think strategically, and work with others to initiate changes will depend on it. The competitive advantage of the organization will rely on how the leader will effectively make strides to benchmark what is good for the organization.

Provoking Question:

How are your improving your business acumen?

Don't You Trust Me?

"It takes 20 years to build a reputation and 5 minutes to ruin it" **– Warren Buffett**

Trust is not given, it is earned. When it comes to making decisions, others need to have trust in what you say. This is only accomplished by consistency and integrity. As a new leader, what you say and what you do must always be in alignment. When you establish trustworthiness, others relinquish their authority to you. Understand, trust is provided by the person who is influenced, not by the influencer. It is never built on what a leader is going to do, but what they have already repeatedly done. There must be a track record.

People might say when they first meet someone, aren't we trying to establish trust? Yes, but the initial phase of the action is curiosity or testing, not trust. Trust is a mandatory attributes for a leader and members of the organization. People at all levels must integrate and establish a foundation of trust in each other on multiple matters to be effective. Well intended requests or actions that undermine trust can have serious consequences and ramifications on operations, opportunities, and advancements for all concerned.

When people do not trust their leaders, they are much more likely to leave their positions. Organizations experiencing high turnover rates can be caused by many issues, but certainly one of them is a lack of trust. Regardless of the problem, trust falls into the core of it. Leaders assuming positions of authority must determine what are the potential problems they could encounter amongst team members, seniors, executives, and colleagues as a whole and identify if they are trust related.

Before determining these other areas, new and emerging leaders should first conduct a self-assessment to determine their level of trustworthiness. This does not imply that you look into the mirror and ask, "Don't you trust me?", but to bring the team together and have open and honest dialogue to understand what they think and how they view each other. What are their greatest concerns and perceptions of you? Another option is to invite an external 3D party to gather the data. You might be surprised at what you find.

What causes distrust of a leader and what are some other solutions? They are:

- **Lying -** Once a lie has been told by a leader, it becomes very difficult if not impossible to regain a trusting relationship. If the relationship is structured on mistrust or the initiation of a lie, then the foundation of the association crumbles. Leaders, especially new ones must recognize that others gather information simply by being at the right place and time. Usually, this is obtained outside of the organizations structured flow of communication. **Solution:** Reputation is everything to a new or emerging leader. Once a leader is deemed a liar, it is almost impossible to gain that trust back. Ensure all communication is provided with honesty and forthrightness. Never let your word be brought into question.
- **Withholding Information -** Leaders must always keep teams informed of what is happening. Now, here is where it becomes a touchy matter for leaders. All information is relevant information contingent upon what the information is and who actually needs to know it. Leaders must be cautious about information dissemination. **Solution:** If information cannot be disseminated to the group as a whole due to security,

incompleteness, or other pending circumstances, then simply state that fact. Then inform them that you will let them know as soon as possible once it becomes available. Providing what you know now prevents vital information from being delivered too late. Information should come directly from the leader, not from outside or 3D party sources. The more informed people are, the better they feel about their role in the organization and the more trusted the leader becomes.

- **Transparency** - Leaders should consider the knowledge being distributed amongst teams. There must be clear communication of information, objectives, agendas, goals, and intent within the organization. When teams gather and share thoughts or ideas, they must have a clear spectrum of the vision and details of their role in its achievement. When teams feel mislead by the leader or openness is diminished, mistrust evolves. **Solution:** Information travels faster than ever amongst members. Leaders must stay ahead of their information pipelines to prevent misinformation from spreading. Information flow is like a leaking faucet at night; once it drips, everybody hears it. Providing updates, instructions, and information directly, honestly, and timely prevents employees from feeling betrayed or mislead.

- **Gossip** - It is never a good practice to discuss matters of a personal or professional nature regarding others in a public forum or even in private forum with individuals who do not have a need for that knowledge. This type of behavior communicates to all workers at all levels of an organization that the leader does not care about them. **Solution:** Concern yourself with matters that are in direct relation to the work at hand and others well-being. Situations that deal with the individual's privacy or violations of that privacy should only be discussed with the individual in particular, or with those who are in a need to know position. This should be an issue of organizational policy and the leaders code of ethical behavior.
- **Unethical Behavior** - Leaders are bound by ethics. When a leader attempts to enforce regulations, values, or moral codes on employees that are in line with the organizations, but fails to comply with them themselves is actually an enforcement of mistrust. **Solution:** Ensure that what you say and

what you do are in alignment. Employees trust leaders whose actions are consistent with what they say. New leaders must hold themselves and others accountable to the same standards.

A leader and their team need to have a stable connection and an established relationship of trust at all times. It takes time for a team to understand and agree on this concept; however, it is a necessity. If members are regularly joined and can adopt this behavior, trust will evolve and strengthen. A leader without trustworthiness is simply a member of the team with a title; all voice and no volume. Trust is the high-octane fuel of leadership.

Provoking Question:

Just how trustworthy are you as a leader?

Hold 'em or Fold 'em

"Ideas pull the trigger, but instinct loads the gun"
– Don Marquis

Kenny Rogers wrote a song called, *The Gambler*, where he sang about the life of a card player. The lyric goes, *"... every gambler knows that the secret to surviving is knowing what to throw away and knowing what to keep."* The same concept applies to new leaders. There are times when they have great ideas they believe will propel them, the team, and the organization to the next level. However, if the idea doesn't generate the level of buy-in needed, the leader must decide if the idea will cause a waste of resources or if they should keep the idea and fight for it. Playing cards for money is like making decisions about ideas, you can either hold 'em or fold 'em.

Leaders who are most effective are the ones who are always engaged in thought. They spend their time being creative with new ideas, concepts and perspectives to change systems that currently exist to create a better outcome or new ones all together. New leaders should adopt this methodology because it creates a habit of consistency and generates an ongoing practice of innovation. Remember, just as a poker player decides what cards to keep based on what enters their hand, so the new or emerging leader decides on what to promote and what to discard based on the ideas that enter their mind.

The most important thing today in business and, for that matter, the world are ideas. As mentioned in, *Focus or Flatline,* ideas have strength. They are the cornerstone of creativeness, but unfortunately, some new leaders are stuck in the managerial mindset without a blueprint to guide them into thought leadership or stratospheric thinking. They often require a strategy to transition from managerial maintenance to leadership innovation. Many new leaders just entering the role have hundreds if not thousands of ideas bouncing around in their head. As far as their ideas, they should *hold 'em* and try to identify their core message. If the idea doesn't merit consideration for the long-term benefit of others... then *fold 'em.*

Ideas, no matter how well intended, cannot help everyone. For this reason, new leaders must be conscious of who they are trying to help and how to help them. Having an idea or message that is not appealing to a specific market is a recipe for destruction. Having a plan that does not specify a target niche ends up helping very few people or none at all. By clarifying your idea, you avoid confusion of its intent and as a result, you can play your hand out based on its potential to achieve the desired outcome. We see a world of possibilities and ideas are the platform for those possibilities. To quote comedy writer and author, Robert Orben, *"We have enough people to tell it like it is, now we could use a few who tell it like it can be Alpha* work in their present circumstances, but live in the future of their ideas.

Provoking Question:

What will you do with your ideas; hold 'em or fold 'em?

Decisions for Decades

"Don't ever make decisions based on fear. Make decisions based on hope and possibility. Make decisions based on what should happen, not on what shouldn't."
- **Michelle Obama**

Leaders, especially those entering leadership roles for the first time, must understand the difference between power and authority. When making decisions it is always best to have as much information as possible. It is a good practice to invite others into the decision-making process to garner advice and gain multiple perspectives to obtain a viable solution.

The Military has a decision-making program called the M.D.M.P (Military Decision-Making Process). It is an analytical approach to problem solving. Much in this way, leaders should consult specialist or subject matter experts to assess merits of a situation and arrive at potential options for a decision. They are referred to as consultants. The leader's decisions made today can have an effect that lasts for decades.

Exceptional leaders never make a decision that affect others without some form of consultation. Even those who are not in leadership roles have something to contribute. Everyone has something to learn from the experience. In Roger Fisher and Alan Sharp's book, *Getting it Done: How to lead when you're not in charge*, they write, *"Team members are more likely to adopt a new way of doing things if each participated in the meeting were past performance was reviewed and changes formulated. Having everyone take part in thinking improves the quality of the thinking."* This statement provides value in having multiple voices of input, but it does NOT imply that everyone makes the decision jointly. The leader must announce the intended focus to the group, but with the goal of learning and contributing. In *Smart Leaders Smarter Teams*, Roger Schwarz writes, *"To benefit fully from mutual learning, the whole team needs to share the mindset."*

The decision-making process is much like a board game. If you want to play the game, you need certain components. These components are the Pieces, the Rules, the Board, the Players, and the Objective. Let's describe them briefly:

- **The Pieces:** These are the tools and process that are used to make decisions. We might refer to them as systems.
- **The Rules:** You must know that there are regulations or structures that cannot be

violated. This is the hardest aspect to grasp because there are two forms. Written rules which are spelled out in policy and unwritten rules which are derived by culture, habit, circumstances, or history.

- **The Board:** This has to do with positioning. Leaders must recognize their level of influence in the process and maneuver properly in accordance with specified rules and regulations. New leaders must be prepared to take advantage of opportunities immediately because their window may only be open for a short time.
- **The Players:** They are the members involved in the process of making the decision. They can be referred to as the *stakeholders*. Having multiple options that can lead to the desired outcome gives the leaders varying perspectives.
- **The Objective:** This is the final component which refers to the desired outcome. This level of the game is the center of the entire process for which all the other components come into play.

New leaders should accept the idea that compromise does not mean conformity. When making a decision, understand the facts, consider various solutions and their consequences, make sure that the decision is consistent with your objectives, and effectively communicate your final conclusion. Making decisions that go against the norm is not always easy, however, it should not compromise your principles. When the greater picture is seen and communicated to everyone of what the end will look like, the process becomes less complex.

Provoking Question:

How will your leadership decisions today affect future leaders tomorrow?

CHAPTER 6
Calling All ALPHAs

Calling All ALPHAs

Most of the great leaders of history were people just like you. They were not necessarily smarter, wiser, or more gifted than you are, but they had a resilience for serving others that was motivated by a purpose and a sense of destiny. They identified, embraced, developed and maximize their leadership potential.

We as leaders of the 21st century, whether new or emerging, have a moral obligation to build, inspire, develop, and challenge other leaders to become better than they believe themselves to be. This, in itself, is a massive undertaking: however, with knowledge, motivation, and focus, leaders can usher in a new era of better leaders.

This current decade and decades to come will cultivate a new group of thinkers. We call them... *millennial's*. We must decide how we're going to develop them mentally; not so much of what they will do, but how they will think and who they will become. Society and businesses as a whole are transitioning from information processing to stratospheric thinking. The need to gather old and new leaders of all industries together to forge forward and create a better world through improved thinking is critical.

Average leaders must begin to think and perform like exceptional leaders. They must become the Alphas. New forms of partnerships and alliances now link organizations together across all segments and with these partnerships comes the inevitability that we must deal with challenges that new leaders will encounter. Today, part of every leader's job, whether in business, government, or private enterprise is to help people see the full value of what they contribute and how the leaders' nurture them in the Alpha philosophy.

Provoking Question:

Who will you help become the Alpha of tomorrow?

ABOUT THE AUTHOR

Terry Budget is the Founder and CEO of the keynote speaking, training, and consulting firm Alpha Success, LLC. He served 21 years of active federal service with the United States Army consisting of tours in Kuwait and Iraq. Terry was awarded the Bronze Star Medal for meritorious service in a combat zone to include the Meritorious Service Medal accompanied with multiple other awards.

He was the top graduate in his graduating class from the University of Phoenix with a Master's degree in Management. His academic knowledge includes training in human resource management, negotiations, and leadership from University of Villanova, Capella University and University of Notre Dame. He is also a member of the Delta Mu Delta International Honor Society in Business Administration and holds the Corporate Speaker designation from the International Association of Corporate Speakers.

Terry has been a speaker and trainer of leadership for over 20 years. His specific ideas about leadership stems from combat experience, intensive studies, corporate work experience, and interaction with business owners across the country. These experiences and foundational knowledge formed his

A.L.P.H.A. philosophy: **A**ttitude, **L**eadership, **P**urpose, **H**onor, and **A**cumen.

TESTIMONIALS

Terry reveals the key components to becoming an exceptional leader through practical application and high-level thinking. He does a masterful job of dissecting the Alpha mind and empowers those who desire to move from average to exceptional influencers. *The Leader's Blueprint* is an absolute MUST READ for leaders and managers at all levels.

Brian Delmaso
CEO and Managing Partner, Matrix Success Network

Infectious leadership! First, leadership is affecting behavior. Terry takes it to the next level of infecting behavior. He structures the environment, makes the message transferable, creates contagiousness, an encourages and epidemic of getting results. Read this book and do the same.

Phil Sorentino
Co-Founder, Humor Consulting

The Leader's Blueprint: How Average Leaders become Alphas...and Why <u>You</u> Should Too" is an excellent read and well executed. The "Connection" Infection as a concept gets right to the point! The wisdom found in these pages are timeless. This is a must have reference for every emerging leader.

Valarie Ghant
Director, Center for Multicultural Student Services, James Madison University

"This book will teach you how to become a 21st century leader by harnessing the power of your mind. I highly recommend it"

Steve Siebold
Author of Secrets Self-Made Millionaires Teach Their Kids and How Rich People Think

Terry hit it out of the park. Our global community needs now more than ever NEW leaders with NEW thinking to help tackle some of the toughest issues that our communities face. This book helps to unlock the right mindset to achieve your goals.

Chris V. Rey
Mayor of Spring Lake, North Carolina

"Terry Budget has managed to use creative parallels and prose to bring to life his leadership experiences, the good, bad and lessons learned! The Leader's Blueprint, is a well-articulated step by step guide that meticulously breaks down the art of winning for young and mature leaders. Before anyone considers taking on a new leadership role or transforming their teams, *The Leader's Blueprint,* is a must read!"

Dawn Nicole
Personal Branding Global Leader, CEO of The GrowGetters

In Terry's new book, *The Leader's Blueprint,* I believe he has captured what will continue to be a Leadership premise going forward. He coins the phrase *Stratospheric Thinking.* In his reveal, I understood this to mean, nothing is possible until it has been realized in the mind, outside your current paradigms and then physically accomplished. He also made a statement I know in my soul is true as well; "*Your association will determine your destination.*" Make every effort to associate with the right people.

Sam Slay
Leadership Speaker and author of Work Jockey

Made in the USA
Monee, IL
19 March 2020